T0207594

Dark Poems and Stories of Sahel

Inspiration of Edgar Allen Poe

SAHEL PARSA

AuthorHouse™
1663 Liberty Drive
Bloomington, IN 47403
www.authorhouse.com
Phone: 833-262-8899

Because of the dynamic nature of the Internet, any web addresses or links contained in this book may have changed since publication and may no longer be valid. The views expressed in this work are solely those of the author and do not necessarily reflect the views of the publisher, and the publisher hereby disclaims any responsibility for them.

Any people depicted in stock imagery provided by Getty Images are models, and such images are being used for illustrative purposes only.
Certain stock imagery © Getty Images.

This book is printed on acid-free paper.

ISBN: 979-8-8230-0985-0 (sc)
979-8-8230-0984-3 (e)

Library of Congress Control Number: 2023910830

Print information available on the last page.

Published by AuthorHouse 06/27/2023

authorHOUSE®

Contents

Transition of Old Life to New

Moonlight shining through

Chained upon the table with blood dripping
from wrists down the satin cross.

Caught in the cup of immortality

Blood soaked white gown

Screaming of agony

The sacrifice of oneself to gain
a new life with true love

True Love Awaits

Wrist upon wrist

Blood in blood

Transformation through the hearts of one

Eyes are locked

Key is immortality

Trust

A wolf in sheep's skin he is

He might be breathing behind your neck

Your neighbor

Your friend

Or even a lover

All you know is that he is waiting for you

Dracula

Give me immortal living

I trade my soul for power

I have endured torture and war

I am the only soul ruler

I am the son of the Dragon

Darkness so cold within

The skin is cold as ice

The eyes are deep red as fresh oozing blood

The smell is like a dead rose

The veins of their arms are as vines through
an old, battered gate in an abandoned garden

Immortality is No Longer a Sin

Cup of eternity

You could feel the love through the spell

As both hold hands while the blood dripples
from their wrists into the cup of eternity

They repeat the curse, the moon,
the blood, and the sacrifice

Strigoi

Blood red

Moonlight shines in the night

Rich blood

Skin so cold

Fangs sharp

Skin like snow

Lycanthrope

The human becomes the wolf

Full Moon is the predator, and the werewolf is the prey

The werewolf is locked in chains enslaved to the moon

The werewolf howls for love as he craves the comfort he needs.

Halloween Bash

It's Halloween night, the ghosts gather, witches on their brooms, the monsters come out underneath the beds, they hunt during the night with the moon and stars gleaming the night. Trick or treaters pass through the houses on the right and left begging for treats to fill their bag to the tippy top. The little ones eat their candy until their bellies become the shape of a pumpkin.

Death by Suicide

Drip drop

All my blood

Look at all the mess you have made

Death has come because of you

Don't look at me upon a frown

Look at me upon a smile

Bed Bugs do Bite

The monster in the closet

The monster under the bed

It's really in their head

Charon

When there is death

One sees death

Death will be there

Death will be near

Death has come

No one will stop the reaper

Down I Go

I painted the roses red

Now cut off my head

Take me down the rabbit hole

Let me drop dead

The Death Gift

From life to death

To the dead living

One life is exchanged for another

Being reborn,

Reincarnated some might say

Or is it a curse to live while others die in front of your eyes

One might say it's the gift we all crave to have

Power and strength with immortality that runs through your blood

God like you can say

Italian Farmer

An immortal man buried in cement within the
ground in all places Ojai Valley California

Vladimir is the name or even Ambrogio, maybe even Dracula.
As they thought he must be long dead, but one can't die if they
are of immortal blood. Luckily, he is guarded by his beloved
friend the hell hound. Looking, searching, calling for his true
love through the cement above. Recalling the moments he
became trapped, he dreams of the night he pushed his love
toward Hades' palace due to his thirst not just for blood but
for power. I am here my love he screams in agony in pain dried
up as a prune with little to no blood left. As the reincarnated
love of Vladimir is calling to him in her dreams as she is not
understanding why she knows this man and feels that he needs
her. She has been seeing herself in modern times becoming
immortal with his blood ruling many lands again as his queen
beside his throne. He will escape and come back soon. She
recalls that she had these dreams since she could remember as
this always was her destiny as she had no choice. Her connection
is too strong and cannot be broken. But this is all in her dream,
so she doesn't know if he is truly trapped and still there. She
packs up and goes with no map but only memories to guide
her. She reaches the spot, but he cannot be found. The coffin
is empty, and she hears a snarl right behind her. Maybe the
whole time the hell hound was really in disguise as he is known
to shape shift so one doesn't know you might be sitting next to
him right now or maybe he is your friend, teacher, or even boss.
Basically, he is out there like everyone else looking for love.

Murder Filled with Blood

Drip Drop

Blood all around

Hands dripping with blood

Eyes shut

Nightmare comes to life

The Protector

Tap Tap

Awoken to the glass-stained window shaking

Appears to be a black crow waiting for an answer

Go out the porch viewing the crow still staring deep into the soul

Snap!!!

A stick is broken under the bare foot

Crow turns around red bloodshot eyes; he attacks shooing away the intruder that is right behind

Transforms into this beautiful man who she recognizes

He is the one in the painting that hangs above the fireplace that's been there for centuries

Dark Tall Predator

Lecture hall it is today

Take the front seat

Seems like nothing new

Wait why is that man here

He was in my other class too

He can't just have added, it's the middle of the semester

Class ends after everlasting lectures; I rush to my car looking behind, it's him again.

Wait he is gone, but appears in front of my car and calls me a name that I have heard before

Wait, I know him, he was the one who drank my blood from the club

Why did I forget

Did he take away the memories, the pain, the suffering?

Golden Mask

Close my eyes

Darkness I see

Appears a man in golden mask

A death mask to be exact dripped in gold

Sitting upon a red throne

Surrounded by men who bend down to their ruler

Death

I open the door, and a strange man asks for a cup of water. I tell the man to come in and wait in the living room. He tells me that I'm too kind, and something just kicks in and I ask him you're not here for water. He nods and asks where it happened. I point to the bottom of the stairs. He says he is very sorry but it's my time to go. He lifts his hood back on and grabs the scythe. He opens the door, and a boat awaits to take me on my journey into the underworld where Hades rules.

Pomegranate Seed

Hades filled with fire

Guarded heavily by his trustful hellhounds

He waits for a new love

Persephone is long gone

Spring is known to be all year round in California

He crushes a pomegranate in his hand with the juice that turns into fresh blood, the blood of his new lover who seems to appear in the river upon the boat.

Bell of the Town

Children playing on the grass

Surrounded by beautiful marble stones, some with descriptions, some with no words at all

Bells ringing, where could that be coming from

The church is too far

There is no toy insight with bells

Wait, it can't be the children going closer to the ground trying to hear it again.

Ding Ding Ding!!!!

She was just buried this morning by her husband.

Again, the bells are heard ringing louder and louder as the whole town scrambles to dig up the freshly buried grave.

The man who endured torture awoken from peaceful sleep

Torches so Bright, it almost appears to look like the scorching sun. men from young and old walking on sand struggling to avoid webs and the crawling scorpions. Scarabs all dead scattered through the cold sand. It must be here that a man in white fedora yells. The men smash the walls down. There is a beautiful solid gold sarcophagus. The men lift the heavy top. The man in the fedora grabs a torch and takes a closer look. Reaches for the Ankh Pendant then OH NO a hand reaches for his neck and drains him dry of no blood. The others scream "It's Ambrogio". What everyone thought was just a myth turns out to be real.

A murder waiting to Happen

Blood Blood Blood

It's everywhere

It's on the walls

On the ground

Soaked in the soles of my feet

Was it a dream

Was it a nightmare

No, it was him

The Son of the Dragon

Wolf or Just a daydream

Walking through the dark night

Shadows lurking all around

Howling is heard

It can't be a wolf this is LA

Suddenly in the dark corner a wolf lurks

Staring into my soul, I run, and they run faster, no escape

I am shaking so shaking I trip on a rusted glass bottle then nothing completely disappears.

Door Opens to Close

Life is only the Beginning

Death is the ending

Death is like a locked door that only has one key and the key is life

Wallpaper peeling

Pipes banging in the walls

It must be rats or mice

Scratches on the walls

Red liquid spilling through the walls

Blood must be, the smell of copper pennies fills the air

Pushing against the wall, hearing a living being struggling to breathe

The walls shatter to the ground

Face to face with a decayed corpse

Frost Bitten

The snow has fallen, grab the sleds

The ground suffocated by snow,
yet there are shovels

It is deep under, dig deep to
fill air through lungs

The Man Who Suffered Torture

A beautiful man with ocean blue eyes,
Golden curls has suffered pain
no one has ever endured

A Rock blunged to his head,
dripping down his forehead

Knife slicing down his shoulder
as more blood is drawn

Arrows piercing through veins as he
looks at himself in the mirror and
sees nothing but perfection.

Tool of Power

In the deep dark woods, a body laying
upon dirt drained of blood

Ravenous crows feast on the decaying body.

Being watched by a mysterious dark figure who
knew the soul that once was held in the body

In the hands of the decaying body is a deep ruby red pendant
that holds dark magic that no one should have a grasp on.

The dark figure puts it around his vein popping
neck and the eyes turn solid black as coal.

Thanatos

The Grim Reaper is never shown to grin only with a hood slouched overhead, with a scythe in his hand. Have you ever heard of his origin story, his life before guiding the damned in the five rivers in the underworld. He himself was a living soul as well, he had beating blood pumping veins, a weak mortal body. He was a boy slaved to a Greek merchant not having any clue who he truly was, his whole life he lived as an orphan. He had always asked the gods every day to help break free of his chains. One night he finally was visited by a god but not the one of his choosing. Hades the god of the underworld told him he will break his chains if he works for him. The boy was unsure, not wanting to be a slave again but Hades reassured him that he would have the freedom he had been craving for and could roam the Earth freely if he transported the damned souls to the underworld kingdom. The boy reached out his hand and agreed. Hades handed a black hood and a Scythe to carry for protection from demons as well as hell hounds that live in the kingdom. Hades says, "By the way Thanatos I hope this Death Wish finds you well. You not only wished for this, but you were born for this."

Time is Ticking

Time is tricky

Time is slow

Time is fast

Our bodies are ticking like a clock

Decaying every minute within an hour

Every heartbeat is a second passing by

When it strikes midnight, you will see Death knocking, waiting at your doorway.

I hope these stories won't haunt you in your sleep

Printed in the United States
by Baker & Taylor Publisher Services